GREAT PEOPLE

MOTHER TERESA

Angel of Mercy

written by Anita Ganeri

Ilustrated by Leighton Noyes
and Karen Radford

 hachette INDIA

DIGBY is a treasure collector. Every Saturday he picks up a bargain at Mr Rummage's bric-a-brac stall and loves listening to the story behind his new 'find'.

HESTER is Digby's argumentative nine-year-old sister – and she doesn't believe a word that Mr Rummage says!

Mr RUMMAGE has a stall piled high with many curious objects – and he has a great story to tell about each and every one.

KENZO the barber has a wig or hairpiece for every dressing-up occasion, and is always happy to put his scissors to use!

Rummage's knick-knacks

2

Mrs BILGE pushes her dustcart around the marketplace, picking up litter. Trouble is, she's always throwing away the objects on *Mr Rummage*'s stall...

Mr CLUMPMUGGER has an amazing collection of ancient maps, dusty books and old newspapers in his *Rare Prints* kiosk.

CHRISSY's Genuine Vintage Clothing stand has all the costumes Digby and Hester need to act out the characters in *Mr Rummage*'s stories.

YOUSSEF has travelled far and wide and carries a bag full of souvenirs from his exciting journeys.

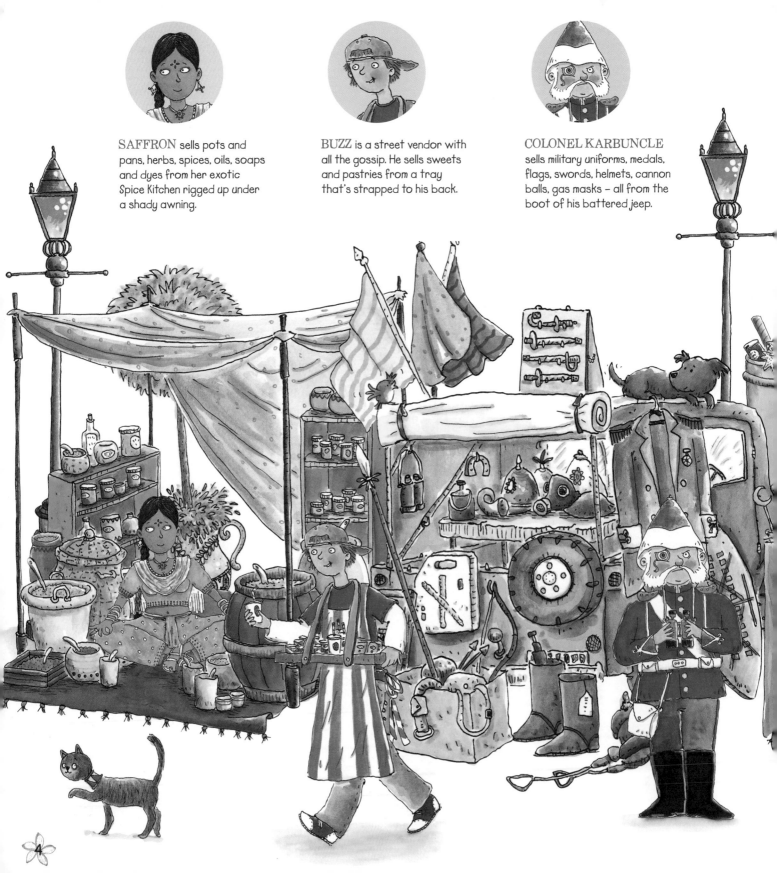

SAFFRON sells pots and pans, herbs, spices, oils, soaps and dyes from her exotic Spice Kitchen rigged up under a shady awning.

BUZZ is a street vendor with all the gossip. He sells sweets and pastries from a tray that's strapped to his back.

COLONEL KARBUNCLE sells military uniforms, medals, flags, swords, helmets, cannon balls, gas masks – all from the boot of his battered jeep.

4

PIXIE the fortune-teller sells incense, lotions and potions, candles, mandalas and crystals inside her exotic New Age tent.

PRU is a dreamer and Hester's best friend. She likes to tag along, especially when make-up and dressing up is involved.

JAKE is Digby's chum. He's got a lively imagination and is always up to mischief.

MR POLLOCK's toyshop is crammed with string puppets, rocking horses, model planes, wooden animals – and he makes them all himself!

Every Saturday morning, Knick-Knack Market comes to life. The street traders are there almost before the sun is up. And by the time you and I have got out of bed, the stalls are built, the boxes opened and all the goods carefully laid out on show.

Objects are piled high. Some are laid out on velvet: precious brooches and jewelled swords. Others stand upright at the back: large framed pictures of very important people, lamps made from tasselled satin, and old-fashioned washstands – the sort that drip when you pour the water in.

And then there are the things that stay in their boxes all day, waiting for the right customer to come along: war medals laid out in straight lines, stopwatches on leather straps and cutlery in polished silver for all those very special occasions.

But Rummage's stall is different. Rummage of Knick-Knack Market has a stall piled high with a higgledy-piggledy jumble of things that no one could ever want. For who'd want to buy a stuffed mouse? Or a broken penknife? Or a pair of false teeth?

Well, Rummage has them all. And, as you can imagine, they don't cost a fortune!

Digby Platt, seven-year-old collector of antiques, was off to see his friend Mr Rummage of Knick-Knack Market.
It was Saturday, and, as usual, Digby's weekly allowance was burning a hole in his pocket.

However, Digby wasn't going to spend his money on any old thing. It had to be something rare and interesting for his collection, something from Mr Rummage's incredible stall.

Hester, Digby's older sister, had come to the market too. She always kept an eye on Digby's visits there. She had secret doubts about the value of Mr Rummage's objects, and felt, for some big-sisterly reason, that she had to stop her little brother from buying 'useless bits of junk'.

As Hester and Digby approached Mr Rummage's stall, they found him hard at work with a duster, polishing a small, battered brass bowl.

'Hi there, kids,' said Rummage, blowing on the bowl and rubbing hard. 'I'll be with you in a moment. I just want to get this bowl nice and shiny for my collection.'

'What are you collecting, Mr Rummage?' asked Hester, suspiciously. Glancing around Rummage's stall, she didn't think he needed any more old junk.

'I'm collecting for charity,' replied Rummage, giving the gleaming bowl one last rub. 'I'm going to put this bowl on the counter, then people can put their spare change in it.'

'It looks a bit battered,' said Digby, peering closely at the bowl. 'Wouldn't a nice, new bowl be better?'

'Oh, but this is no ordinary bowl', said a soft voice from behind him. 'It's an Indian alms bowl.'

'Hi, Saffron,' said Hester. 'What's an, er, alms bowl?'

'It's a bowl holy people use to collect donations of money, food and other things,' replied Saffron, smiling.

'Yes, and this particular alms bowl,' continued Rummage, 'belonged to a very holy person indeed. Her name was Mother Teresa. She became a nun and spent her life helping the poorest people in India and around the world. One of her jobs was to go from house to house collecting leftover food for the poor to eat.'

 # Mother Teresa

Mother Teresa was born Agnes Bojaxhiu on 26 August 1910 in Skopje, a town which today lies in the country known as Macedonia.

Her parents, Nikola and Drana, had three children – Lazar (a boy) – and two girls, Age and Agnes. Agnes was the youngest. Her family called her Gonxha, which means 'flower bud', but later she changed her name to Teresa when she became a nun.

In the 20th century, Mother Teresa became one of the most famous and admired women in the world. In 1948, she founded a religious order of nuns, called the Missionaries of Charity, in Calcutta (now Kolkata), India. Through this order, she dedicated her life to the poor, sick and dying, in India and around the world.

But let's find out more...

An alms bowl is used to collect money and food to give to poor people.

Family life

Agnes's father was a merchant and her family were reasonably well off. Her father owned several houses, and the family lived in one of them. Agnes went to the local primary school, then to secondary school.

Agnes as a young girl.

She did well at her studies and was particularly good at writing and music. But Agnes's happy family life was suddenly shattered in 1919, when her father died.

Agnes's mother couldn't manage the business and the family lost everything, apart from their home. Agnes's mother, a devout Christian, told her children that possessions and belongings weren't important. It was much more important to live an unselfish life. It was a lesson that stayed with Agnes for the rest of her days.

There are many different pictures of Mary, the mother of Jesus

The Roman Catholic Church

The Roman Catholic Church is one of the main branches of Christianity. About half of all Christians today are Roman Catholics. The head of the Roman Catholic Church is the Pope whose headquarters are in the Vatican City in Rome. The word Pope means 'father'. Roman Catholics believe that the Pope takes the place of Jesus' disciple, Peter, who led the first Christians and was the first bishop of Rome. Roman Catholics pray to God, to Jesus and also to the Blessed Virgin Mary, Jesus' mother. Many Roman Catholic churches have statues or pictures of Mary and other saints – people who have lived especially holy lives.

Religious life

Agnes's family were devout Roman Catholics and Agnes's mother tried to put her Christian faith into practice by opening her house to the poor and needy. She and her three children prayed together every evening and attended the local Catholic church, called the Sacred Heart of Jesus. Agnes and her sister sang in the church choir and took part in many church activities.

Certainly, during her early years, Agnes was fascinated by stories of the lives of missionaries, those people who went overseas to help spread the Roman Catholic religion. And by the time she was twelve, she was convinced that she too wanted to commit herself to a religious life.

Montenegro is a country of mountains and lakes

To the mountains

Once a year, the family made a pilgrimage to the shrine of the Madonna of Letnice in the mountains of Montenegro where they prayed in the little chapel. This was also the family's annual holiday and it was hoped that the mountain air would help Agnes's poor health.

Agnes with her brother and sister

'Hmph!' muttered Digby. 'What happened next, Mr Rummage?'

'Well, on 13 October 1928, Agnes and another girl set off from the city of Zagreb on the long train journey across Europe to Paris. Agnes's mother and sister came to wave them off.'

'Did she pass the interview?' asked Hester.

'Yes,' said Rummage. 'Both girls were accepted as novices, or new nuns. From Paris, they were sent to Loreto Abbey near Dublin in Ireland. Agnes never saw her mother again.'

'They must have felt very homesick,' said Hester. 'I mean, they were a long way from home.'

'Yes,' agreed Rummage, 'but they were kept very busy at the Abbey. They had just six weeks to learn English, a language they'd never spoken before. Luckily, Agnes was good at languages and soon picked it up.'

'So how did Agnes become a nun?' asked Hester. 'Are there special nun schools?'

'Not exactly,' chuckled Rummage. 'Agnes applied to join a group of nuns called the Loreto Sisters. She chose them because she knew they already worked in India. And to her great excitement, the Mother Superior invited her for an interview in Paris.'

'I don't know what a Mother Superior is,' said Digby. 'But it sure sounds scary!'

'A Mother Superior's a head nun,' said Hester, looking pleased with herself. 'I saw one in a film.'

The Loreto Sisters

The Order of the Sisters of Loreto, or the Loreto Sisters, is the common name for the Institute of the Blessed Virgin Mary. This order was founded in 1609 by Mary Ward, an English Roman Catholic nun. Mary joined a convent of the Poor Clares in France, but decided that God was calling her to lead a more active life. She began to recruit other nuns to set up and run schools for girls.

Mary was strongly criticized by the Catholic Church because her nuns did not wear habits or live in a convent. But her work continued and, in 1822, the Institute was given a house, outside Dublin, which was named Loreto Abbey. The Order flourished in Ireland and, in 1841, the Loreto Sisters were asked to begin teaching and nursing in India.

Loreto Abbey near Dublin

Mary Ward (1585-1645), the English Roman Catholic nun who founded the Loreto Sisters

Religious orders

The Loreto Sisters are one of several religious orders of nuns in the Roman Catholic Church. Catholic nuns believe that they are 'Brides of Christ' and take vows of poverty, chastity and obedience. They live as part of an order, or religious community.

Some nuns live mainly in a convent and have little contact with the outside world. Others may work as nurses or teachers. Whichever order they belong to, nuns lead strict lives of prayer and self-sacrifice, devoted to God. There are also similar orders for monks.

A rosary is used by Roman Catholics when they pray. It is usually made up of beads and a religious cross. The beads represent different prayers.

'But when did Agnes get to go to India?' asked Hester, impatiently.

'1 December 1928,' said Rummage, 'the two girls left Ireland and began their long journey to India. At that time, there weren't any aeroplanes so they had to go all the way by boat.'

'How long did it take?' asked Digby.

'It took about four weeks,' replied Rummage. 'But Agnes wasn't called Agnes anymore. She'd chosen the name Sister Teresa, after a saint called Teresa of Lisieux. She was a French nun who believed the best way to do God's work was by doing small, simple tasks and doing them cheerfully.'

'Agnes, er, Sister Teresa must have been glad to get there,' said Hester.

'She was,' agreed Rummage. 'But it was very different to what she was used to at home. Her first stop was Colombo in Sri Lanka. She wrote lots of letters to her family, describing the heat, the crowded streets and the tropical palm trees.'

'Look, I've found Colombo!' said Digby, excitedly, pointing to an old globe he'd found on Rummage's stall.

'Excellent, Digby, now can you find Madras (now Chennai) in India?' said Rummage.

'It was there that Sister Teresa was shocked to see how terribly poor the people were. She knew that if people back home could see this poverty, they might stop grumbling about their own problems. Anyway, after a stop in Calcutta, the nuns reached Darjeeling.'

'What did they do there?' asked Hester.

'They spent the next two years learning to live according to the rules of the Loreto Sisters,' said Rummage. 'Just before her twenty-first birthday, Sister Teresa took her vows, or promises, of chastity, poverty and obedience. From then on, there was no going back to her former life.'

British India

In 1928, when Agnes first arrived in India, the country was still being ruled by the British. They had set up the English East India Company in 1600 to trade in Indian goods, such as tea, spices, cotton and indigo.

Gradually, the power of the English East India Company grew and it turned from trading in Indian goods to administrating huge tracts of Indian land.

Soon, large parts of India came under British rule. In 1858, the Company was abolished and the British government took direct control of India. This was the beginning of the British rule, or Raj, as it was known. It continued until August 1947 when India became an independent country.

Life in Darjeeling

Darjeeling was a town in north-east India in the foothills of the Himalayan mountains. Nicknamed the 'Queen of the Hills', it was the town in which many British people spent the hot summer months. Surrounded by tea plantations, it had large houses and splendid hotels, cooling breezes and stunning views. It was also used as the site for a hospital for British troops.

It was in this beautiful setting that Sister Teresa completed her training. She studied religion, read the Bible and learned Hindi and Bengali. She also taught in the convent school and helped in a small hospital where she nursed some of the poorest people. Sister Teresa was remembered as being hardworking and jolly.

An old print of Darjeeling in the 1920s shows workers on a tea plantation

'So where did Sister Teresa go next?' asked Digby.

'She went back to Calcutta,' replied Saffron, taking up the story. 'It's one of the biggest cities in India and now called Kolkata.'

'Got it!' yelled Digby, jabbing his finger at his globe.

'Sister Teresa was sent to work in the Loreto School in the Entally district of east Calcutta. She taught geography and history to the girls.'

'Was she a good teacher?' asked Hester.

'She was,' said Saffron. 'She enjoyed her work and her pupils liked her very much. All the lessons were in English but later she moved to another school, called St Mary's. This school taught girls from poorer backgrounds and the lessons were in Bengali. She must have been happy because she stayed there for 17 years!

Then, in 1935, Sister Teresa went to teach at a primary school in a desperately poor area. She was shocked to see the awful conditions there. But things were even worse in other places. Every Sunday, she visited poor people in the Motijhil slum.'

'What's a slum?' asked Hester.

'It's a very poor and overcrowded part of a city where people live in makeshift huts of tin, mud or even cardboard. Often there's no running water or electricity and no toilets. Life in a slum is very hard indeed.'

Then, on 14 May 1937, she took her final vows and became Mother Teresa. And that's how most people know her.'

Calcutta

The city of Calcutta began as a small village built on swampy marshland along the banks of the Hooghly River. In 1686, British merchants set up a trading post on the site of the village. At first, the post wasn't a success but in 1696, a fort was built and after that, Calcutta grew steadily into a major port.

In 1756, Calcutta was captured by the local ruler, but the British won it back the following year. A much larger fort was built and Calcutta became the capital of British India until 1911. Today, Calcutta is the capital of the state of Bengal and is called Kolkata, its old Bengali name.

In the 1800s and early 1900s, Calcutta had grand buildings

Poverty and palaces

As the capital of British India, Calcutta grew wealthy. It had grand government buildings, together with clubs, hotels and stores for British officials and their families. But not far from these splendid buildings were squalid back streets where the poorest people of the city lived. Even the convent in which Mother Teresa lived was in a large, peaceful compound, a far cry from the stinking slums sprawling just outside its walls.

In the early days of British rule, grand processions were held on the streets of Calcutta

Today, there are still many slum areas in the city

17

'Mother Teresa didn't stay a teacher forever,' Rummage went on. 'Things changed when she fell ill in September 1946. She was sent to Darjeeling to get better but on the train journey, an amazing thing happened.'

'What was that, Mr Rummage?' asked Digby and Hester at the same time.

'Mother Teresa called it "a call within a call",' replied Rummage. 'She was sure she heard God's voice telling her to leave the convent and live among the poorest of the poor. But she needed permission to leave the Loreto Sisters. The Archbishop of Calcutta didn't like the idea of her wandering the streets of Calcutta on her own. He tried to make her change her mind.'

'And did she?' asked Hester.

'Quite the opposite,' smiled Rummage. 'She was more determined than ever! And at last the Church authorities in Delhi agreed to let her leave the Loreto Sisters and work outside the convent. They also agreed that she could still be a nun.'

It was very hard to leave the safety of the Order after so many years. Besides, she had to give up her Loreto habit and find something else to wear! She decided to dress like a Bengali woman. So she went to the market and bought a plain white cotton sari with a blue border, and some simple sandals. She pinned a crucifix to her left shoulder.'

Indian Independence

Independence Day celebrations in India, 1947

Hindu-Muslim violence

In the 1930s and 40s, there was a lot of turmoil in India as many Indians were working hard to win freedom for their country. They wanted the British to leave the government in their hands. But this caused trouble between India's two main religions - Hinduism and Islam. The Muslims were afraid that Hindus would take control of an independent India. They demanded that part of India should become their own country - Pakistan. On Friday, 16 August 1946, Muslims protested on the streets of Calcutta. The result was a bloodbath. Thousands of Hindus and Muslims were killed in the violence.

Partition of India

The British Government decided that the only way to stop the violence was to give India independence. They would also divide the country into Hindu and Muslim parts. At midnight on 14-15 August 1947, India became free. But it was impossible to divide it neatly into Hindu India and Muslim Pakistan.

So the states of Punjab in the west and Bengal in the east were split along religious lines. This left the two mainly Muslim areas - renamed West and East Pakistan - on opposite sides of the country. Many people found themselves on the wrong side of the borders and fled for their lives. In the chaos that followed, millions were killed in Hindu-Muslim violence. Millions more became refugees, many of whom poured into already overcrowded Calcutta.

India was divided into three parts: India, West Pakistan and East Pakistan

*This map is a pictorial representation and not to scale

A place to stay

As Mother Teresa's school became more popular, she needed a bigger building to live and work in. Then she had a stroke of luck. An Indian Roman Catholic, called Michael Gomes, offered her a large room in his home at 14 Creek Lane and it was rent-free.

Poor families flocked to Creek Lane to ask for Mother Teresa's help

Bless this house!

Mother Teresa moved into her new home in February 1949. She brought with her a bench, a box for a table, a chair and a cupboard which she used as an altar. She was also given a bed.

Now, at last, she had a base for her work and space for others to come and join her. Michael Gomes later gave her two larger rooms to use. He was happy to help. He believed that having Mother Teresa in his home was a great blessing.

Food for the poor

When people heard what she was doing, they gave her money and came to help. She also went from door to door, with her alms bowl, asking people for any leftover food to give to the poor and hungry. But Mother Teresa never worried too much about not having enough money or food. She always believed that God would provide her with all that she needed.

'In December 1948, Mother Teresa returned to Calcutta and just before Christmas, she finally began working in the slums,' Rummage continued. 'She decided to start her work in the Motijhil slum which she knew because it was next to her old school of St Mary's.'

'What did she do there?' asked Digby.

'She opened a school for the slum children,' said Rummage. 'Many of them had never been to school before. Often they had to go out to work instead to help their families.'

'That's terrible,' said Hester, quietly. 'What was the school like?'

'Well, it didn't have any classrooms, or even chairs or desks,' Rummage replied. 'In fact, it was just an open space between the huts. The children squatted on the ground and Mother Teresa scratched the letters of the alphabet in the dust with a stick.'

'Did the children like going to school?' asked Digby, doubtfully.

'They loved it,' smiled Rummage.

'There were 21 pupils on the first day, and twice that many the next day. Numbers went up steadily and by January, Mother Teresa had more than 50 pupils and three teachers helping her. Soon she was able to rent a small hut which became a classroom.'

'What other work did Mother Teresa do?' asked Hester.

'Well, she began visiting the many poor and sick people who lived in the slums,' said Rummage. 'It was hard, and sometimes upsetting, work. Once, Mother Teresa met a man with a badly injured thumb. The thumb needed removing, so she took a pair of scissors and cut it off. It's said that the man fainted one way, and Mother Teresa fainted the other! Oh dear, are you feeling okay, Hester? You're looking a bit pale.'

'Do you think Mother Teresa ever got lonely?' asked Hester.

'She might have done but she wasn't on her own for long,' said Saffron, taking up the story. (A customer had come to Rummage's stall and he didn't get many of those.) 'Soon, a girl called Subhasini Das came to join her. She'd been one of Mother Teresa's pupils at St Mary's and, like her teacher, wanted to help the poor. She later took the name of Sister Agnes.

Then, two months later, two more girls followed. They took the names of Sister Gertrude and Sister Margaret Mary. They helped Mother Teresa teach the children in the school, and look after the sick and dying people in the slums.'

'Did they become nuns, too?' asked Digby.

'Yes,' replied Saffron. 'In October 1950, Mother Teresa set up her own order of nuns called the Missionaries of Charity. She became head of the Order, and the girls who joined her were known as "Sisters".'

'Creek Lane must have been getting quite crowded!' said Hester.

'It was,' smiled Saffron. 'Especially as more Sisters joined the Order over the next two years. Soon the house was bursting at the seams. It was clear they needed somewhere bigger to live, but it was difficult finding somewhere cheap enough for them to rent. Of course, Mother Teresa wasn't worried. She was sure that God would help them out.'

'And did he?' asked Digby, eagerly. 'Help them out, I mean?'

'It certainly looked that way,' replied Saffron. 'By chance, Mother Teresa found out about a house at 54/A Lower Circular Road, one the main roads in Calcutta. It was owned by a Muslim man but because of the trouble between Muslims and Hindus, he'd decided to move to Pakistan. He agreed to sell it to the Missionaries of Charity for a low price and they moved in February 1953.

The house became the headquarters of the Missionaries of Charity and was known as the Motherhouse. And, amazingly, it's still the Motherhouse of the Order today.'

Missionaries of Charity

Joining the Order

When a girl joined the Missionaries of Charity, she was expected to devote her life to helping the poor. The nuns wore the same habit as Mother Teresa – a white sari with blue borders and a small crucifix. Apart from this, they had very few belongings – two cotton saris, a pair of sandals, a crucifix, a prayer book, an umbrella, a thin mattress and a metal bucket for washing themselves and their clothes.

A day in the life

The Sisters' days followed a strict routine. They got up at 4.40 am, got washed and dressed, and cleaned their teeth with ash from the kitchen stove. From 5.15 am to 6.45 am, there was morning prayers. For breakfast, they had cold milk and five chapattis and by 7.45 am, they were out at work. At noon, they returned to the Motherhouse for prayers and lunch. Afterwards, they did housework and had a short rest. Then it was back to their duties in the city. At six, they came back for a supper of rice, dal and vegetables. Then there was time for mending and relaxation, until bed at 10 pm.

'Mother Teresa worked very hard,' said Digby.

'Probably,' said Rummage. 'But there was too much work to do to rest. She opened a home where poor and sick people could die in peace. In Calcutta, thousands of people were homeless and lived on the city streets. And that's also where they died, often with no one to look after them.'

'How awful,' said Hester, sadly. 'Why couldn't they go to hospital?'

'Most of the hospitals were full, and besides, these people were too poor to pay for medicines,' said Rummage. 'Mother Teresa wanted somewhere where they could die in peace. Luckily, the city authorities wanted to help,' Rummage went on. 'So they offered her a house next to a temple dedicated to the Hindu goddess, Kali. The house was dirty and run-down but Mother Teresa accepted immediately. She called the home Nirmal Hriday which means the place of the "pure heart".

'It must have been hard to see people dying and in pain,' said Hester.

'It was,' agreed Rummage. 'But Mother Teresa believed that everyone had the right to "die beautifully", to spend their last days feeling loved and looked after.'

'Even then Mother Teresa didn't rest,' smiled Saffron, taking up the story. 'She found another old house, close to the Motherhouse, and turned it into a home for unwanted slum children. She called it Shishu Bhavan, which means "the children's home". It was opened in September 1955, and had space for 90 children.'

'Why did no one want the children?' asked Digby.

'Well, sometimes their parents were too poor to look after them', said Saffron. 'They just couldn't afford food or clothes. And sometimes their parents had died and they were left as orphans.'

Hinduism

Most people in India are Hindus. They follow the ancient religion of Hinduism which began at least 4,000 years ago. Most Hindus believe in a great spirit, called Brahman or God. They also believe in hundreds of gods and goddesses who represent Brahman's many powers. The Kali Temple, close to which Mother Teresa's rest home, Nirmal Hriday, was set up, was one of the holiest places in Calcutta for Hindus.

Kali the goddess

The fierce-looking Kali is the Hindu goddess of death. She stands for the frightening aspects of death and destruction which people must face and overcome. Kali is shown wearing a tiger skin, with fang-like teeth and a necklace of human skulls. Her skin is usually black. The Kalighat temple in Calcutta is her main temple. The temple is one of the 51 *shakti peethas* where different parts of Sati's (another incarnation of Kali) body fell and became holy places of worship. This temple used to have daily animal sacrifices till it was outlawed by animal activists.

Kali, the Hindu goddess of death

An old house in the city of Calcutta was turned into a school

Helping each other

Some of the Hindus weren't happy to have Christian nuns working next to their temple. They were afraid that they would try to convert dying people to Christianity. The Hindu priests organized protests against the Sisters. But when the Sisters took in a dying Hindu priest, they were finally accepted by their neighbours.

Mother Teresa helped many children from the slums

A crippling disease

Leprosy is an infectious disease caused by a bacteria. It deforms parts of the body, and damages the skin and nerves. One of the first signs of the disease are light spots on the skin which may develop into lumps. If the disease is not treated, it can cause paralysis and loss of fingers and toes.

Because these symptoms are so unpleasant, lepers were thought to be unclean and were made to live apart from other people. Millions of people still suffer from leprosy, particularly in poorer countries, such as India. But the disease can be treated with drugs if it is caught early, and many people have been cured.

Mother Teresa visited hospitals and gave comfort to the sick and dying

'However, there was another group of people whom Mother Teresa wanted to help,' continued Saffron. 'And they needed her help very badly.'

'And who were they?' asked Hester.

'They were lepers,' replied Saffron. 'People who suffer from a disease called leprosy. At that time, many people were frightened of lepers in case they caught the disease themselves. So lepers often had to leave their homes and live apart from other people. They had no jobs, so they were forced to beg on the streets. Many were so ashamed of their illness, they tried to hide away.'

'Poor people,' said Digby, softly. 'Was Mother Teresa able to help them?'

'She was, Digby,' said Saffron. 'She opened a shelter for lepers at Gobra on the edge of the city. But it only had space for about 150 of the 30,000 lepers in Calcutta. A few months later, she set up a clinic at Shishu Bhavan where lepers could come to get medicine to treat their disease. Soon afterwards, the shelter at Gobra was closed down because the land was needed for building. Mother Teresa tried desperately to find a place somewhere else but it wasn't easy. Nobody wanted lepers living close by.'

'So what did she do?' asked Hester. 'She couldn't let all those people down.'

'She set up a mobile leprosy clinic instead!' said Saffron. 'With a donation of money, she bought two vans and kitted them out with medicines and food. The vans drove around the slums, handing out the medicine.'

'What a brilliant idea!' said Digby. 'That way lots of people were helped.'

'But Mother Teresa still wanted a permanent place where lepers could live and work,' Saffron went on. 'The Missionaries of Charity were already working at a leper community at Titagarh on the outskirts of Calcutta and Mother Teresa was given some land to build a new clinic there. Even so, another community was badly needed.

Then Mother Teresa had a stroke of luck. The Indian Government gave her a large plot of land about 320 kilometres from Calcutta. She raffled a car given to her by the Pope to raise funds, and began to build a leper community. She called it Shanti Nagar, which means "the place of peace".

Here, hundreds of lepers were able to live normal lives. They helped to build their own houses, grew their own rice and ran their own grocer's shop. They also made baskets for sale and even started a printing press. This meant they did not have to beg and could look after themselves.'

Awards and Prizes

Lotuses and jewels

Throughout the 1960s and 1970s, Mother Teresa received many awards and prizes from governments and organizations around the world, and from the Pope in Rome. Among the most precious were those awarded by the Indian government for her work among the Indian people.

Mother Teresa meets the Pope in Rome, Italy

In 1962, Mother Teresa was awarded the prestigious Padma Shree, one of the highest honours given to Indian citizens. In 1980, came an even greater honour. Mother Teresa was awarded the Bharat Ratna, India's highest civilian award. This award recognizes 'public service of the highest order'.

Nobel Peace Prize

Mother Teresa receives the Nobel Peace Prize

The Nobel Peace Prize is awarded every year to a person who has worked hard to make the world a peaceful place. In 1979, Mother Teresa won the prize and a cheque for £90,000. This was set aside to build more houses for lepers.

Special celebrations

In December, she flew to Oslo in Norway for the glittering prize-giving ceremony – wearing her simple cotton sari and sandals, as usual, Mother Teresa said that she herself was unworthy of the prize but accepted it on behalf of 'the poorest of the poor of the world'.

Afterwards, she asked for a banquet in her honour to be cancelled and the money given to the poor. The celebrations didn't end there. When she arrived back in India, a reception was held for her in the Red Fort in Delhi. Only three other people from India had received the Nobel prize before and after her – Rabindranath Tagore, Sir CV Raman and Amartya Sen.

'Did Mother Teresa ever get a holiday from work?' asked Digby.

'Not exactly a holiday,' smiled Rummage, taking up the story. 'But in 1960, she went to the USA. It was her first trip outside India. After that, she visited Britain, Germany, Switzerland and Italy, promoting her work and raising funds.'

'She was quite a globetrotter, then' said Hester.

'Yes, indeed, Hester,' said Rummage. 'And the trip was just the beginning.

She spent the rest of her life travelling to different countries, making speeches, accepting awards and opening new houses.'

'She must have become very famous,' said Digby.

'She did,' agreed Rummage. 'And in 1969, she became more famous still. A British journalist, called Malcolm Muggeridge, came to Calcutta to make a film about her work. The film was called *Something Beautiful for God*. When this film was shown, Mother Teresa became a superstar!'

'Did being famous make her different?' asked Hester. 'Sometimes it goes to people's heads.'

'No,' said Rummage. 'She was always very humble. When someone asked her about the amazing work she had done, she replied it was God's work, not hers.'

'I wish I'd been able to meet Mother Teresa,' sighed Digby. 'I wonder what she was really like.'

'I wish I'd met her, too,' said Rummage. 'She's always been a great heroine of mine. She was only tiny – about four and a half feet tall – but she was incredibly energetic and strong-willed. Some of the places she visited were dangerous, so she also had to be very brave. Once she visited the Middle East during a war between the Israelis and Palestinians. There, she persuaded the two sides to stop fighting just long enough for her to rescue 37 patients from a hospital!'

'I could never have done that,' said Hester, admiringly.

'That's for sure,' laughed Digby. 'You're scared even of spiders!'

'When people asked Mother Teresa where she got her courage from, she said she got it from God,' said Rummage.

'She believed that God guided her in all she did. She once said "I am like a little pencil in God's hand. He does the thinking. He does the writing. The pencil has only to be allowed to be used".'

'Did everyone like her?' asked Hester. 'Or did some people think she was a goody-goody?'

'Good question, Hester,' said Rummage. 'Some people didn't like Mother Teresa. They said that, for all her good work, she didn't do anything to try to get rid of poverty once and for all. They also criticized the poor medical care in her houses and the fact that she was so busy travelling she didn't have time to get involved with poor people any more.'

'What did Mother Teresa say to that?' asked Digby.

'She genuinely felt she was doing God's work,' said Rummage. 'So she took no notice of the criticism. She used to say "No matter who says what, you should accept it with a smile and do your own work".'

Worldwide Work

Missionaries abroad

At first, the Missionaries of Charity were only allowed to work in Calcutta. Later, they opened houses in other Indian cities, such as Delhi and Mumbai where there were also slums. In 1965, the Pope gave Mother Teresa permission to open houses in other countries. The first was opened in Venezuela and many more soon followed in Africa, Australia, Asia, North America and Europe.

In 1980, a house was opened in Skopje, Mother Teresa's hometown. It was difficult for the Sisters to live so far from home. Many felt homesick and struggled to get used to a different language and culture. Even so, Mother Teresa expected them to do their work cheerfully and willingly.

Missionary Brothers

In 1963, a new branch of the Missionaries of Charity was founded. It was called the Missionary Brothers of Charity. The two Orders worked closely together.

The first Brothers were priests who lived in Shishu Bhavan, the children's home in Calcutta. They looked after homeless boys living in the city's railway stations. Later, they took over the running of the Titagarh leper community. The head of the Brothers was an Australian priest, called Father Andrew. His helpers wore ordinary shirts and trousers, instead of religious dress. A small crucifix pinned to their shirts was all that showed they were Brothers.

The Missionaries of Charity has spread all over the world

Mother Teresa dies

Despite years of hard work, Mother Teresa seemed unstoppable. Although she was frail and bent, and often ill, she always returned to her work. When she asked why she did not rest more, she replied, 'There will be plenty of time to rest in eternity. Here there is so much to do.'

But in 1983, she suffered heart problems during a visit to Pope John Paul II in Rome and was forced to rest. After this, her health became more fragile and she often took ill.

Sister Nirmala

By 1996, Mother Teresa was seriously ill and elections were held to decide who would take over as head of the Order. Sister Nirmala was chosen as the new leader. She was 63 years old, kind and wise, and came from a Hindu family in Nepal. Mother Teresa was very pleased with the choice.

Mother Teresa's grave

Mother Teresa's funeral ceremony.

State funeral

Despite her ill health, Mother Teresa visited Rome and the USA again in May 1997. It was to be her last tour. On 5 September 1997, a few days after her eighty-seventh birthday, Mother Teresa died of a heart attack. Hearing the news, the French president said, 'This evening, there is less love, less compassion, less light in the world'.

A week later, she was given a state funeral, which was a great honour. Her body was carried through the streets of Calcutta on a gun carriage, as thousands of people watched from the roadside. Leaders from all over the world attended the funeral mass which was held in a sports stadium. Afterwards, Mother Teresa was laid to rest beneath a simple stone slab in the Motherhouse.

'It's very sad she died,' said Hester. 'But what an amazing life she'd led. I mean, she started off as a simple nun and went on to become world famous!'

'Exactly,' said Rummage. 'And even though everyone missed her terribly, the work of the Missionaries of Charity went on after her death. And it still goes on today. There are now 600 houses in 130 countries, and about 4,500 Sisters, 400 Brothers and thousands of other helpers. They still help poor people and lepers, but they also help the homeless, drug addicts, victims of war and people with AIDS.

'Right, that's it,' said Digby, firmly. 'I've decided.'

'What now?' said Hester, suspiciously.

'I'm not going to buy anything this week,' said Digby, dropping his pocket money into the alms bowl. 'I'm giving my money to charity instead.'

'Goody-goody,' muttered Hester.

'Very generous,' said Rummage, rattling the bowl which was filling up nicely. 'And now, you two, Saffron and I must get back to work. So goodbye, until next week. I'll see you next Saturday for another story.'

'Bye, Mr Rummage! Bye, Saffron!' called Digby.

'Bye!' said Hester, quickly dropping some coins into the alms bowl before anyone noticed.

The making of a saint

What is a saint?

For Christians, a saint is someone who's led an especially holy life and perhaps suffered for his or her religion. Some Christians pray to the saints and ask them for help and guidance. They also celebrate Saints' Days. Some saints are linked with particular jobs, events or places. For example, St George is the national saint of England.

The Vatican

The coat of arms of the Vatican City, Rome, in Italy – home of the Roman Catholic Church and the Pope.

Canonization

In the Roman Catholic Church, some holy people are declared to be saints or canonized, after their death. There are several steps to becoming a saint.

The process usually begins five years after the person's death. Local bishops investigate the person's life and send their findings to the Vatican in Rome.

A group of cardinals (senior priests) and other scholars approve the findings.

Then the Pope declares the person to be 'Venerable', which means that they are a role model of Roman Catholic qualities and virtues.

The next step is to find out if the person performed a miracle after his or her death. If they did, they are beatified and then given the title of 'Blessed'.

To finally become a saint, there needs to be proof of a second miracle performed after the person's death.

Schoolchildren remember Mother Teresa in their prayers

Blessed Teresa of Calcutta

While she was alive, many people called Mother Teresa a living saint because of the good works she did. After her death in 1997, the Roman Catholic Church began the process of canonization to make her a saint.

First they needed to find a miracle performed by Mother Teresa after her death. In 2002, they discovered that an Indian woman had been cured of an illness by wearing a locket containing Mother Teresa's picture.

On 19 October 2003, Mother Teresa was officially beatified by Pope John Paul II and became the Blessed Teresa of Calcutta. The Pope said, 'There is no doubt that the new Blessed was one of the greatest missionaries of the twentieth century. The Lord made this simple woman, who came from one of Europe's poorest regions, a chosen instrument to proclaim the Gospel to the entire world – not by preaching but by daily acts of love towards the poorest of the poor.'

A second miracle is needed before Mother Teresa can be made a saint.

Mother Teresa's legacy

A simple person

Agnes Bojaxhiu was born in one of the poorest and most politically unstable parts of Europe. A frail but deeply religious child, she left her home and family to follow her calling of becoming a nun and working among the world's poorest people.

By the end her life, she was seen by many people as a living saint, someone who saw 'the image of God' in each person's face. From her humble beginnings, she went on to help and influence millions of people through her extraordinary and inspiring life.

From her early days in India, Mother Teresa dedicated her life to helping people who were shunned or neglected by society. These included the poorest of the poor, people who were homeless and dying, and people suffering from terrible diseases. Inspired by her firm belief in God, she tried to make their lives more bearable by showing them love and care when no one else would.

Wherever she went, Mother Teresa never shied away from difficult or unpleasant situations. Today, the Missionaries of Charity continue her work around the world, bringing hope and comfort to millions of desperate people.

Life is...

When she was in her seventies, Mother Teresa summed up her own attitude to life:

'Life is an opportunity, benefit from it.

Life is beauty, admire it.

Life is bliss, taste it.

Life is a dream, realize it.

Life is a challenge, meet it.

Life is costly, care for it.

Life is wealth, keep it.

Life is love, enjoy it.

Life is a promise, fulfill it.

Life is sorrow, overcome it.

Life is a song, sing it.

Life is a struggle, accept it.

Life is an adventure, dare it.

Life is luck, make it.

Life is too precious, do not destroy it.

Life is life, fight for it!'